**DEAR PEN PAL**
The Musical

Music & Book
by Annie Brown

**CHARACTERS**

**(all roles in the show are written to be able to be gender bent!)**

**LIAM WILLIAMS**- A nervous but determined individual. SARAH's brother and secret pen pal. Romanticizes everything and struggles to admit he's ever wrong *(alt- name leah, she/her)*

**JO**- a disaster of a human. Receives themself as a pen pal and keeps quiet about it. Hold one deep dark secret that can be decided by the cast upon production. *(non-binary role)*

**SARAH WILLIAMS**- a go getter. Liam's sister and secret pen pal. Has a bad case of senior-idis even though she is only in 8th grade and dreams of the bigger and better future she has in store. *(alt- name Seth, he/him)*

**MAISIE THOMAS**- A pushover that only desires acceptance and to connect with their pen pal (SAM) in a deep and personal way. Loathed by her classmates. *(alt- name Mason, he/him)*

**SKY NELSON**- loves to write and does not hide it. Oftentimes overlooked as an individual. TYLERS's secret pen pal. Loud and outgoing but constantly interrupted. *(non-binary role)*

**TYLER JONES**- super down to earth and real. Just wants a good grade and that is about it. SKY's secret pen pal. *(alt- name Sydney, she/her)*

**SAM MITCHELL**- super quirky and is OBSESSED with bugs and all things related. MAISIE's secret pen pal *(non-binary role)*

**MS. RUPUS**- 8th grade teacher

**A NOTE: JO's big secret is to be decided by the cast and director upon production. This allows room for the cast to make it as wacky or relatable as they desire!**

**MUSICAL NUMBERS**

**PART I**

*(lights come up on an empty eighth grade classroom consisting of desks for students and a larger one belonging to Ms. Rupus.)*

### TYLER

Uh… hi! My name is Tyler, I am 13 years old, and I go to Green Meadows Middle School. Pretty basic right? I mean even the name of my school sounds straight out of a book!

*( A school bell sounds as the classroom fills with students, THE INTRO begins playing)*

### TYLER

As an eighth grader, i'd say my life is pretty normal! All of our lives are! We live in a cookie cutter town with cookie cutter houses, cookie cutter schools, and the same, old, boring, cookie cutter assignments- well that's with the exception of this one, but we'll get to that in a sec.

These are my classmates! We're all pretty good friends… *(a pause as the music stops)* well, we haven't always been. Let me take you back a few months… September 3rd… *(TODAY begins)* the little day that changed it all, letter day!


### MAISIE

STARING AT THE CLOCK WONDERING WHAT COMES NEXT

WILL I EVER GET THE CHANCE, THE CHANCE TO OPEN IT

THE LETTER FROM MY PEN PAL THAT'S FOR MAISIE MAE

OH I KNOW, IT'LL BE TODAY

TODAY


### SARAH

TODAY! I GUESS I PROB'LY SHOULD HAVE STARTED BY NOW

BUT IT'S ALREADY SEVENTH HOUR HOLY COW

TRYING HARD TO DO IT NOW BEFORE IT'S DUE


**BOTH**

AND ALL FOR YOU


**ALL**

DEAR PEN PAL DEAR FRIEND DEAR ONCE IN A LIFETIME CHANCE

TO BE WHO I WANT TO BE


**JO**

WHO CARES IF I'M LATE


**SKY**

OR BAD AT UNO


**LIAM**

OR DATING


**ALL**

I CAN JUST BE THE REAL TRUE ME


**MAISIE**

THE ME WHO DANCES BUT WON'T TELL A SOUL


**JO**

THE ME WHO ONLY JAMS TO ROCK AND ROLL

**SKY**

WITH LETTERS LIKE SHAKESPEARE


**SAM**

BUG COLLECTIONS


**TYLER**

DEAD FROGS


**ALL**

I CAN BE WHO I WANT TO BE


**JO**

So, I'm going to be entirely honest with you all, I have no idea what is going on.

Like of course i get the assignment and everything but… there's a catch!

<u>My partner is myself!</u>

That sounds weird, let me explain!


SO I DON'T KNOW HOW TO DO THIS THIS ASSIGNMENT BY MISS RUPUS

YES, I KNOW IT SEEMS SO EASY BUT IT'S WHAT YOU DON'T KNOW

AS WE DREW THEM FROM THE HAT

I WAS SHOCKED AND TAKEN BACK

BECAUSE THE LETTER THAT I HELD WAS FROM JO

SO I KNOW WHAT YOU ARE THINKING

WHAT'S THE FUN IN SITTING DRINKING PUNCH

WHILE OTHER STUDENTS GET TO HAVE FUN WRITING

WELL THERE ARE SECRETS THAT I HOLD IN PAGES

MADE OF PAPER PENS AND TAPE THAT

PEOPLE IN THIS CLASS SHOULD NEVER SEE


**ALL**

DEAR PEN PAL DEAR FRIEND DEAR ONCE IN A LIFETIME CHANCE

TO BE WHO I WANT TO BE


**MAISIE**

I TURNED IT IN


**ALL**

LATE


**MAISIE**

WELL IN SO NOW I JUST SIT AND

**ALL**

WAIT… FOR THE


**SKY**

NOVELS

**TYLER**

POEMS


**SARAH**

LIES


**LIAM**

CHANCE TO SHARE MY FEELINGS


**MAISIE**

CHANCE TO SHARE MY LIFE


**SAM & JO**

AND TO FIND THE MEANING


**ALL**

I KNOW IT WON'T BE LONG 'CAUSE IT'LL BE TODAY

TODAY

TODAY

TODAY!

*(the song ends as the students return to their seats and frantically begin working on*

*their next letter)*

**LIAM**

*(whispering to MAISIE)*

Hey, hey, HEY! Are our letters due today?


**MAISIE**

*(annoyed)*

Maybe if you didn't lose your schedule you'd know…


**LIAM**

*(to SAM now)*

Gosh… what's up with her?


**SKY**

Hey, where's Ms. Rupus-


**ALL**

*(annoyed)*

SHHHHH!

**SARAH**

*(to audience)*

So you're probably wondering what the heck is going on here. We are officially 3 weeks

into the stupidest assignment I have ever received. Not gonna lie, it seemed okay the

first week! Anonymous pen pals! Woo! Anonymous letters! Woo! Yeah right… I just

don't get the hype. Seriously, we have 8 more months before they ship us off to high

school and what're we doing with that time? We are spending it writing letters.

ANONYMOUS letters that are graded based on effort. How does that even work?

Listen, I have places to go, people to see, things to do beyond  (mocking) "a fun way to

begin the 8th grade". Listen up Ms. Rupus… I don't like you! I said it! I mean like… I

wouldn't actually say that to her because ehhhhh that'd be scary and she'd become all

judgey and fail me and give me detention and It would go on my permanent record and

Yale would not be a possibility and I might just, DIE! (Beat)

Anyway… Where was I, letters, letters, letters, class, rupus, *(spotting audience)* OH!

YOU! Basically we write to each other. Easy enough right? Too easy.9

Let me introduce the class to you real quick, all of the eligible "pen pal bachelors" if you

will…

First we have Maisie over here, to keep this short and semi-sweet, she is clingy but has

no-one to cling to, so that makes her… Maisie. Sky likes to write… too much. Ty is

always the leader of every single group project… take that how you want to. Sam really

REALLY likes bugs... That's my brother Liam…

**LIAM**

Oh, be quiet Sarah, nobody wants to hear your blabbering!


**SARAH**

Make that my <u>annoying</u> brother Liam... and that is Jo who... is a mess... but hey, we all

are, we are in 8th grade after all!

8th grade…

You know, why is 8th grade even essential! I can read! I can write!… well better than

them! This is absolutely useless! But you know... you do what you have to do! Like my

mom always told me, you work for the end goal, not for what surrounds you in the

present. You work hard for your DREAM!

*(GIRL ON TV begins)*


I SAW FROM THE FIRST DAY I RECALL

THAT IN LIFE YOU WILL ALWAYS SEEM SMALL

IF YOU SIT ON YOUR ASS-ETS

AND DON'T SHOW THE CLASS-ETS

THAT YOU CAN BE TALL


WHEN I STARTED AT THIS SCHOOL I JUST KNEW, I JUST KNEW

THAT I WOULD FLY HIGH, WELL HIGHER THAN THE REST

SO I STUDIED THE NUMBERS, ALL THE NOTES, AND ALL THE BOOKS

BUT EACH TIME THERE'S AN ASSIGNMENT IT'S JUST ONE THING IN MY WAY

OF THE HOPES AND DREAMS I FIGHT FOR IN CLASS EVERY SINGLE DAY

ALL THE HOPE THAT MAYBE ONE DAY I COULD STAND UP TALL  AND SAY


IM THAT GIRL ON T.V. WHO DELIVERS THE WEATHER I KNOW YOUR IMPRESSED

BY MY COLLECTION OF SWEATERS

I WAKE UP REAL EARLY

POINT AT SCREENS AND SHARE LISTS

CAUSE IT'S ME, I'M YOUR METEOROLOGIST


We have clear and sunny skies ahead for Sarah Williams as she emerges from the eighth grade with a class rank of 1! Maybe out of 7, but still, she is unstoppable, bound for success, yale better watch out because this future meteorologist is coming! Nothing but sunshine in her forward cast,  Sarah Williams, that's me!


IM THAT GIRL ON T.V. WHO DELIVERS THE WEATHER

I KNOW IT'S WEIRD TO KNOW A LOCAL CELEBRITY

BUT I'M HERE, I CAN HELP YOU THROUGH THE

WINTER, SUMMER, SNOW, RAIN, AND CRAZY WEATHER

WHEN TO WEAR A COAT AND WHEN TO WEAR A SWEATER

CAUSE IT WILL BE ME WHEN YOU NEED A

METEOROLOGIST

-GIST

-GIST

*(letter writing continues. JO stands up and heads towards Ms. Rupus's desk to sharpen*

*his pencil but is stopped by SKY. With a dramatic and nearly judgemental look, SKY*

*covers their paper in the fear of JO seeing their letter and ruining the assignment)*


**SKY**

*(defensively)*

HEY!


**JO**

*(dull pencil in hand)*

Oh, i was just trying to-


*(SKY hmms and gives JO the hand. JO is motioned back to their seat by SKY and they*

*confusingly follow suit.)*


**JO**

you know, it's so funny seeing everybody getting so protective over these letters! As if

knowing another person's pen pal assignment would be "the end of the world"! These

letters are what they look forward to every day! Ha, imagine... couldn't be me... *(sadly)*

couldn't be me... but hey! There's nothing wrong with a bit of self expression right? I

<u>enjoy</u> writing to myself! I do! I'm the only one who ever sees my letters, therefore, why

not use that to my advantage! Why not use it as a place to vent, to write down all my thoughts, all my secrets! Sucks to be them because they have to play the "get to know me" game and filter what they are writing, not me! Just Jo over here cheating the system heheh.

**TYLER**

*(writing)*

"Dear pen pal, I"- uh I don't really know what to say. All I keep getting in these letters is more of the same! I mean how am I even supposed to respond to there letters when all they are are short-

**SKY**

STORIES! It was a dark and stormy night in the town of-

*(THE BUG SONG starts, interrupting SKY)*

**SKY**

Hey!

**MAISIE**

I'M NORM'LY NOT THE TYPE TO JUST TALK ALOUD

BUT IT THINK THIS IS A

CHANCE FOR ME TO STEP UP AND TALK ABOUT

WHAT IT IS THAT MAKES ME ME! MI MI!

Get it? Like the notes? Like do re mi…? Anyways!


PEN PAL I THINK WE COULD BE BEST OF FRIENDS

NOT LIKE I HAVE MANY

BUT I THINK THAT THROUGH THIS ASSIGNMENT WE

CAN BE, CAN BECAUSE

SOMETIMES YOU JUST NEED A FRIEND

A FRIEND TO HELP YOU GET BY, TO THE VERY END

A SPECIAL FRIEND TO BE THERE FOR ME

WHAT DO YOU THINK?


With love, your pen pal!


**SAM**

I REALLY LIKE BUGS AND I LIKE TO GO FOR WALKS

I LIKE TO SIT IN THE SUN

I SPEND ALL MY DAYS DRAWING PICTURES OF BUGS THAT, NEVER GET DONE


**(INSERT BUG JOKE, ACTORS CHOICE)**


**MAISIE**

SO YOU GOT ANY HOBBIES?

**SAM**

BUGS!


**MAISIE**

AND IN YOUR FREETIME?


**SAM**

I LIKE BUGS!


**MAISIE**

SURELY THERE'S GOTTA BE MORE TO YOU!


**SAM**

Well- I collect mugs!


**SAM**

WITH PICTURES OF BUGS

BUGS!

I LOVE BUGS!

BUGS

BUGS

BUGS

SOMETIMES

BUGS

I REALLY LIKE BUGS

HELP YOU FIND

MORE BUGS MORE BUGS

BUGS


**MAISIE**

CAUSE SOMETIMES YOU JUST NEED A FRIEND


A FRIEND TO HELP YOU GET BY TO THE VERY END


A SPECIAL FRIEND TO BE THERE FOR ME AND TO HELP YOU  FIND


THE MEANING OF LIFE


THE MEANING OF LIFE


THE MEANING OF


LIFE

**JO**

*(writing)*

dear "jo" (*laughs*), it's jo... how ya doing bud? Bacakaroo! Best friend! (*Laughs thinking they are SO funny, to audience still laughing*) get it, because, because it's myself... just... (*brushing it off and pulling it together as the audience doesn't react*) anyways... this gets pretty boring I'm not gonna lie, I like to sprinkle in some juicy things every once in a while though! Ya know, for myself to read. Like the fact that sometimes my mom lets me drive our golf cart even though I'm not 16, or... or the fact that I don't like chocolate! Controversial, I know, it's one of the main topics we argue about in letters! (*Chuckles*) that's about it though! (*Pause, admitting to the audience on the verge of a confession, vulnerable*) well- there's also this one thing... one of my deepest darkest secrets! Something so so so secret that only the letters I write to myself will ever get to know... (pause) woah woah woah, I know what you're thinking, "just spill the beans jo" but nope! Won't do it! Can't a guy(gal) keep something private for once in his(her) life! That's why I LOVE this assignment! I get to sit back and relax as well as get everything off of my chest... what could be...


**SKY**

BETTER! I made it better! (*Clears throat*) it was a dark and SPOOKY night in the-


**LIAM**

*(interrupting SKY, to the audience)*

You know what I just love? Like, love love? Like more than anything else in the whole entire world love… *(a pause)* LOVE! *(giggle)* just everything about it! *(playing it cool)* Now, i'm quite the ladies man, and I know what you're thinking, "Liam… look at you! Are you really" but I am, I am, I promise I am. I mean, next to my <u>stellar</u> looks, it's the smooth moves, the carefully crafted words I say that make the girls go WILD! Like… *(spotting SKY)* like watch this… *(to SKY)* uh, hey! Sky! Can a borrow a pe-

**SKY**

No.

**LIAM**

But I-

**SKY**

nope!

**LIAM**

Well, well okay maybe it doesn't work 100% of the time… or ever, but hey I really really want it to and you know if you want something bad enough it's bound to happen right? I just want love! And to be entirely honest, aside from Sky, I may have found it, but hey how many times have you thought you loved somebody you actually didn't?

*(music starts)*

I really REALLY want to be hopeful… but then I think about the others!


**LIAM**

I MET A GIRL IN A STARBUCKS PARKING LOT

WE HIT IT OFF LIKE TWO PEAS IN A POD

BUT WHEN SHE SAID GOODBYE, I SAID SEE YOU LATER

TO FIND OUT THAT KATE WAS A PEA HATER

SO I HEADED HOME AND NOW I KNOW

THAT SHES JUST ONE OF THE GIRLS

I THOUGHT I LOVED BUT ACT'LY DIDN'T LOVE

YEAH SHE'S JUST ONE OF THE GIRLS I LOVE


THEN THERE WAS GRACE STUDENT BODY PRESIDENT

SHE HAD THE FACE OF MARILYN MONROE

SO I GAVE HER SOME DIAMONDS A GIRLS BEST FRIEND

TO FIND OUT THAT THERE WAS ANOTHER MAN

SO I SWING AND I MISS AND I ADD TO THE LIST OF THE

GIRLS I THOUGHT I LOVED BUT ACT'LY DIDNT LOVE YEAH  SHE JUST ONE OF

THE GIRLS I LOVED

BUT THEN THERES HER THE GIRL WHO READS MY LETTERS

I KNOW IT'S WEIRD BUT THERES A CONNECTION HERE

YEAH SHES THE GIRL I READ FROM WRITE TO AND LOVE


YEAH SHES NOT ONE OF HE GIRLS I THOUGHT I LOVED BUT ACT'LY DIDN'T

LOVE

YEAH SHE THE GIRL I LOVE


**SKY**

IT WAS A-

*(Lights out)*


**SKY**

*(In the dark)*

HEY- no!!! This is my time to shine

*(A single spot comes on downstage, sky marches into it)*

THANK YOU! *(Calming down)* Thank you. You see…


*(Speechless starts)*


all I want to do is share my stories! Is that so so hard to do!


I TRIED TO DO THIS CALMLY TRIED NOT TO SING

I TRIED TO JUST TALK NOW IS THAT SUCH A HARD THING  TO DO

WELL NOT FOR YOU

I WRITE ALL THESE STORIES I SPEND ALL MY TIME

I POUR OUT MY HEART AND SOUL IN EV'RY LINE

BUT EV'RY TIME I SPEAK I FEEL IM NOT THERE

I TALK BUT IT SEEMS YOU DON'T CARE


CAUSE YOU SNICKER AND LAUGH AND YOU CALL ME A FOOL

YOU PUSH ME AROUND AND USE ME AS A TOOL

I THINK THAT ITS TIME FOR ME TO STAND UP AND SING

AND SHARE THIS THING


It was a dark and stormy night in the middle of a small Rhode Island town as Abigail made her way through the dark and spooky forest. As she took a step the leaves crunched under her feet but she could not hear them for her head was filled with the sounds of the ghosts surrounding her


**ALL**

*(sporadically, as ghosts)*

boo boo boo boo boo!


*(at this moment JO once again stands to sharpen their pencil after their first failed*

*attempt)*

**SKY**

Fearful of what was ahead of her on this endeavour, she questioned whether she should continue on her journey. She took one more step when all of the sudden she looked up and saw nothing else but-


**JO**

THE BINDER! *(gasp)*


*(THE BINDER SONG begins, interrupting SKY)*


**LIAM**

OH MY GOSH IS THAT REALLY IT


**SARAH**

OF COURSE IT IS BUT THIS SORT OF FEELS MORE LIKE A SKIT


**MAISIE**

I WISH I WAS DREAMING


**JO**

OR THIS WAS SOME SORT OF PRANK

**ALL**

BUT IT'S THERE, IT'S RIGHT THERE


**TYLER**

AND NOW I WANNA


**MAISIE**

Hey! let's be smart here, is that really the BEST idea I mean-


**TYLER**

LOOK AT IT NOTHING IS TELLING US NO

**JO**

I AM!


**TYLER**

SO WHY DON'T WE JUST PICK IT UP AND GIVE IT A GO


**JO & MAISIE**

NO!


**SARAH**

ITS SITTING THERE AND LOOKING LONELY AND SCARED

**LIAM**

AND I AM SINGLE AS  CAN BE AND I AM TURNING THE BIG  ONE-THREE AND

THIS IS MY ONLY WAY OUT


**SARAH**

WOAH!


**MAISIE**

Sarah is right, what do you mean "your only way out"? Were young, were free, and we

do NOT need to open that binder to feel something!


**LIAM**

but you don't understand, what I have with my pen pal it's, it's LOVE!  I mean, I know it

sounds crazy but this is different than anything I've ever had before, she is different!


CAUSE I'M TOO YOUNG FOR KIM AND I AM TOO SHORT FOR  LIZZY

BUT MY PEN PAL RIGHT HERE

THINKS THAT I AM THE SHIZZY

MY PEN PAL IT'S LIKE SHE FINALLY SEES ME

MY PEN PAL


**SKY**

I mean what's to say your pen pal is a "she"?

                    **LIAM**

BLEH


                    **JO**

I mean, is there something wrong with that?


                    **LIAM**

 no, no, it's not that, it's just, it's just...

I don't know what to think...


                    **SARAH**

I think… we just open it already


                    **LIAM**

me too


                    **SAM**

ME THREE


                 **MAISIE & JO**

NO

**MAISIE**

I mean let's think, is that really the best idea


SERIOUSLY HAVE WE TRIED OUR BEST

WE RUN THE RISK OF SUSPENSION BY JUST CROSSING THIS DESK

I THINK IT'D BE BETTER IF WE JUST SIT DOWN


**SARAH**

BUT THERE ARE SECRETS THAT ARE KEPT THAT

WILL STAY QUIET IF NOT LEPT AT BY THIS

OPPORTUNITY


**MAISIE**

SO MAYBE WE DON'T

MS RUPUS SEEMS BUSY


**LIAM**

AND YOU THINK THAT I CARE


**JO**

HEY LISTEN UP MISTER "SHIZZY" WE SHOULD JUST STAY CALM AND FORGET

THIS WHOLE THING, CAUSE THEY CAN'T KNOW

**ALL (EXCEPT JO)**

NOVELS POEMS LIES

CHANCE TO SHARE MY FEELINGS

CHANCE TO SHARE MY LIFE AND TO FIND THE MEANING


**JO**

THEY CAN'T KNOW

I WISH THEY COULD, THEY CAN'T KNOW

IT WOULD DO ME NO GOOD, CAUSE


**ALL**

I KNOW IT WON'T BE LONG CAUSE IT'LL BE TODAY

TODAY

TODAY

TODAY


*(lights out, end of PART I)*

**PART II**

*(lights come up as everybody is in a panic surrounding MS RUPUS's desk. They are all chattering over each other in an intense debate over "to open or not to open".*

#### MAISIE

What in your right mind makes you think it's okay to open that?

#### TYLER

I mean what's wrong with it? Ms. Rupus left it out and she still hasn't shown up yet!

#### LIAM

Yeah! It's been more than 15 minutes so legally we can leave!

#### SARAH

LIAM!

#### JO

I say we leave it be! You don't know what kind of personal info could be in those letters!

#### MAISIE

*(searching for a new excuse)*

YES! What happened to our fourth amendment ladies and gentleman!

*(the class once again breaks into a roar of chatter and debate. While everybody is distracted, LIAM grabs the binder and dashes away from the crowd with it. Everybody notices and surrounds him with the exception of JO who is in a panic in the corner.)*


**TYLER**

*(grabbing everybody's attention)*

woah woah woah! Lets sort this out, we open the binder, I read it off line by line SLOWLY, and THEN we comment.


**SARAH**

*(loudly)*

But why should you get to be the one to read it?


**MAISIE**

Sarah has a point, if we are gonna do funny business, at least it should be fair.


*(Pause, everybody simultaneously turns their head to look at JO in a panic in the corner of the room. In a rush, TYLER hands JO the notebook as everybody rushes him to stand on a chair in the middle of the classroom)*

**JO**

uh- uh- okay… well pairings I guess first…


**LIAM**

*(to audience)*

this is it…


**JO**:

Sky was with Tyler


**LIAM**:

my true love revealed…


**JO**:

Sam was with Maisie


**LIAM**

the love of my life is…!


**JO**

Liam and Sarah

**LIAM**

MY SISTER??


(A moment of silence as everyone slowly turns to look at him)


**LIAM**

NO NO NO! I mean- uh- pshhhh, I knew that


**SARAH**

what?


**LIAM**

(*nervously*)

Pranked ya! April fools!


**SAM**

it's August,


**LIAM**

no I-


(THE GIRLS I DIDN'T LOVE REPRISE begins, in a panic)

I KNOW WHAT IT LOOKS LIKE IT'S NOT LIKE THAT THOUGH

YOU SEE ME PLAN ALL ALONG HAS FINALLY SHOWN

MY SISTER, MY SISTER HA LOOK AT THAT THOUGH

CAUSE I KNEW ALL ALONG

SO I SAID LETS BE STRONG

LET'S BE WRONG AND TRICK HER

THAT'S WHAT I DID


YEAH YOU'RE JUST ONE OF THE GIRLS

<u>YOU</u> THOUGHT I LOVED BUT ACT'LY DIDNT LOVE

YEAH YOU'RE JUST ONE OF THE GIRLS

I THOUGHT I LOVED BUT ACT'LY DIDNT LOVE NO YOURE NOT

ONE OF THE GIRLS I LOVED


*(awkward silence)*


**ALL**

*(falling for his excuse)*

Oooooooh


**LIAM**

okay so book aside, you know my story, my secrets about my letters, I think it's only fair you share yours aloud!

(Simultaneously)

| | |
|---|---|
| **JO** | **SKY** |
| NO bad idea can't I just read them I mean, | (continues writing and muttering as she writes) |
| **SARAH** | **TYLER** |
| how does this make any sense, who did jo have then, I don't believe it you're not that smart | well I don't have any secrets why am I being dragged into this I- |
| | **SAM** |
| **MAISIE** | I mean mine was kinda given away right away, you know I talked about ants, and worms, and butterflies, and snails, and… |
| hey, hey , hey lets just calm down everyone we don't need to, | |

**MAISIE**

HEY! Make a circle, and let's settle this!

*(Everyone makes a preschool style, criss-cross applesauce, circle in the floor in shock that the pushover raised her voice)*


**MAISIE**

What makes you guys think this is any way to act, teacher or no teacher. This is crazy! This assignment was supposed to bring us together, not tear us apart, but look what we've done!


*(silence as everybody sits shamefully)*


**TYLER**

*(breaking the silence and trying to be understanding)* you know, Sky, I didn't <u>hate</u> your stories! Yes, they were a little long and hard to read at points but they were in fact... stories!...


**SKY**

*(nervously feeling the need to go next)* well, well... LIAM! I didn't mean to reject you that harshly earlier, I don't hate you, you just smell kinda bad.


**ALL**

*(nodding) mmhmm... yep... uh huh...*


**MAISIE**

(interrupting)

Well… uh… that's a start…

**TYLER**

Well what do you want us to say! You're the one who started this "honesty circle" thing, what did you expect.

**MAISIE**

I just want everybody to be themself! After all, that's all that any of us wanted from this assignment! We've spent all of middle school trying to be this picture perfect puzzle piece that fits it with the rest and it took some stupid assignment for us to even see that wasn't at all who we are. So who are you? Really?

**TYLER**

(sarcastically)

Well why don't you tell us "Ms. Perfect"

(*STARTING OVER* beings)

**MAISIE**

Oh, uh, well… I guess I could go first...

**MAISIE**

I HAVE AN OLD SOUL, I DON'T TALK TO STRANGERS

I SIT IN THE BACK, I LEARN NAMES AND FACES

I DON'T TALK TOO LOUD

I KEEP TO MYSELF I-


I TRY SO HARD FOR YOU TO SEE IM HERE

I'M TRYING TO BE WHAT YOU NEED ME TO BE

BUT NOW I SEE THAT YOU DON'T CARE


SO THIS IS WHEN WE ALL SHOULD JUST START OVER

THE POINT WE SHOULD FORGET WHO WE WERE

WHO WE ARE AND WHO WE'RE TRYING TO BE

JUST FORGET ABOUT THE THINGS WE HAVE SAID

FOR THEY WERE SAID WHEN WE WERE IN OUR HEAD

SO LET IT JUST BE

LIAM, AND SARAH, AND JO, SKY, TY, SAM,

AND ME


**SARAH**

I THINK SHE IS RIGHT LETS GIVE IT A WHIRL

CAUSE THERE ARE THINGS YOU DON'T KNOW BOUT THIS COOL GIRL

I LIKE TO CHASE STORM CLOUDS PUT THEM IN MY BOOK

AND WHEN THE STORMS OVER IT JUST TAKES A LOOK TO KNOW

I CAN BE THE GREATEST METEOROLOGIST IN HISTORY

I CAN SEE BRIGHT AND SUNNY SKIES FOR ME


SO THIS IS THE TIME WE SHOULD ALL START OVER

AND SHARE WHO WE REALLY ARE

WHO WE WANTED TO BE AND IF WE'VE GOTTEN FAR


FORGET ABOUT THE THINGS THAT WE'VE SAID

FOR THEY WERE SAID WHEN WE WERE IN OUR HEADS

SO LET IT JUST BE


**+LIAM**

LIAM


**+MAISIE**

AND MAISIE


**+JO**

AND JO


**ALL**

SKY, TY, SAM


**TYLER**

IM SECRETLY LACTOSE INTOLERANT

THAT'S WHY I DON'T LIKE CHEESE


**ALL**

HE DON'T LIKE CHEESE


**SARAH**

I WANNA MOVE TO SAN FRANCISCO

THOUGH I DON'T LIKE THE BEACH


**ALL**

NO, NO, NO, BEACH


**SAM**

I ONLY LIKE BUGS CAUSE OF MY DEAD MOM

HER FAVORITE BUG WAS A LADY BUG


**ALL**

I GOT THESE SECRETS THAT I CAN'T HIDE


**SARAH**

I LIKE TO EAT CHEESE FRIES

**TYLER**

I HAD A PET FROG ONCE THAT I ACCIDENTALLY KILLED


**ALL OTHERS**

THESE LETTERS I THOUGHT WERE PRETTY GREAT


**JO**

*(CONFESSES "BIG SECRET" AND AND ONE CHARACTER REACTS)*


**ALL**

WOOOO


SO THIS IS THE TIME WHEN WE ALL START OVER

AND SHARE WHO WE HAVE BEEN ALL ALONG

SHARE WHO WE WANTED TO BE WHO WE THINK THAT WE ARE


FORGET ABOUT THE THINGS THAT WE SAID

FOR THEY WERE SAID WHEN WE WERE IN OUR HEAD

SO LET IT JUST BE

LIAM, AND SARAH, AND JO, SKY, TY, SAM,

MAISIE, THE SECRETS AND THINGS WE HELD IN

CAUSE WE CAN FINALLY BE FREE AND BE

YOU YOU YOU YOU YOU YOU YOU YOU, YOU, YOU, YOU,

AND ME!


**TYLER**

Ms Rupus is coming!


**LIAM**

well I say we bring the room back to normal and just don't mention it to her! We'll know but she'll never have to!


("Clean up" commences)


**MAISIE**

righty-o


**SARAH**

aye-aye


**SAM**

Okie dokie


**TYLER**

sounds good

                                          **SKY**

sounds snazzy


                                          **JO**

uh- *(later than everybody else and in a panic)* yeah...


                                        **Ms. Rupus**

ah, sorry I'm late! Got a little caught up in the copy room! Did I miss anything fun?


                                     *(Finale begins)*


                                          **ALL**

                                          OOOH


                                          **JO**

oh nothing too crazy Ms. Rupus, just a little class bonding! Anyways, we are ready to

turn in today's letter whenever you are!


                                        **Ms. Rupus**

I am so ready!


                                          **ALL**

                                     WE SHARED THE

**SKY**

NOVELS


**TYLER**

POEMS


**SARAH**

LIES


**LIAM**

CHANCE TO SHARE MY FEELINGS


**MAISIE**

CHANCE TO SHARE MY LIFE


**SAM & JO**

AND TO FIND THE MEANING


**ALL**

CHANCE TO REALLY SHARE

WHO I WANT TO BE-ECAUSE

I KNOW IT WON'T BE LONG CAUSE IT'LL BE TODAY

TODAY

TODAY

TODAY!


*(end)*

# The Introduction

# Today

star-ing at the clock wond'-ring what comes next will I ev-er get the chance the chance to
op-en it that lett er from my pen pal just for mai-sie mae oh I know

it'-ll be to-day to day - - - to-
day I guess I prob'-ly should have start-ed by now but its al-read-y sev-enth-ho-ur

20
+ MAISIE
4
V.
ho-ly cow - try-ing hard to do it now be - fore it's due and all for
Pno.
Vc.
Vn.

ALL

V.
Pno.
Vc.
Vn.
dear pen pal dear friend dear once in a life time chance

to be who I want to be - - - - Who cares if I'm late or bad at

V.
U-no or dat-ing    I    can just be the real true me  -  -  the  me who dan - ces  but
Pno.
Vc.
Vn.

wont tell a soul the me who on - ly jams to rock and roll With
V.
Pno.
Vc.
Vn.

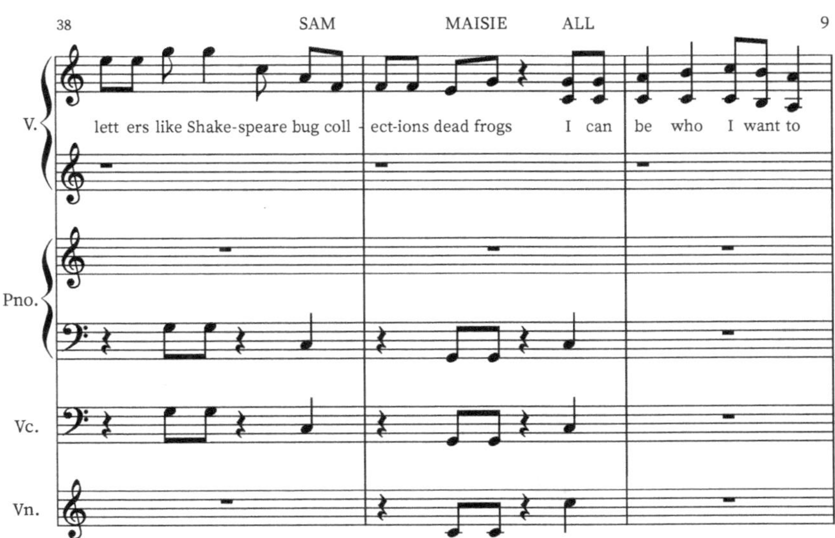
SAM
MAISIE
ALL
lett ers like Shake-speare bug coll - ect-ions dead frogs   I   can   be   who   I want to
V.
Pno.
Vc.
Vn.

41
V.
be - - - bum bum bum bum bum bum
1st- monologue
2nd- this line
so i dont know how to do this this ass - ign-ment by Ms. Ru-pus Yes! I
Pno.
Vc.
Vn.

bum bum bum ooo - - wah bum bum bum
know it seems so ea-sy but it's what you don't know as we drew them from a hat I was
V.
Pno.
Vc.
Vn.

V.
bum bum    bum      bum bum    bum    ooo - wah
shocked and tak - en back be-cause-the lett-er that  I held was from  JO  -  so I
Pno.
Vc.
Vn.

bum bum    wah         bum bum    wah
know what you are think - ing whats the    fun  in  sitt - ing drink - ing punch while

V.
bum bum    bum    ooo - wah         bum bum    bum
oth-er students    get to have fun    wri - i - thing-well there are    sec-rets that    I hold in page-es
Pno.
Vc.
Vn.

55
V.
bum bum bum bum bum bum ooo -
made of pap - er pens and tape that peo-ple in this class should nev-er see -
Pno.
Vc.
Vn.

wah dear pen pal dear friend dear once in a life time chance
- - dear pen pal dear friend dear once in a life time chance
V.
Pno.
Vc.
Vn.

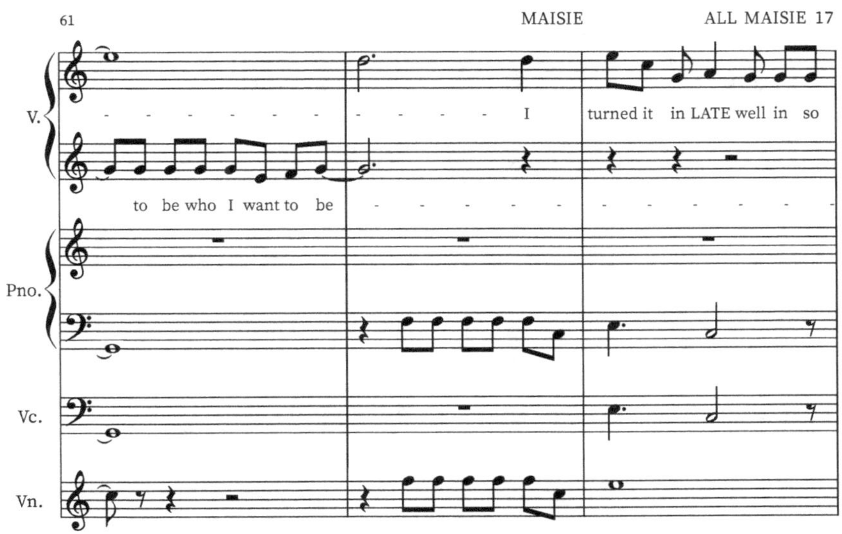
V.
- - - - - - - I turned it in LATE well in so
to be who I want to be - - - - - -
Pno.
Vc.
Vn.

V.
now I just sit and wait - - - - - for the nov - els po - ems
- - - wait - - - - - - - -
Pno.
Vc.
Vn.

V.
lies chance to share my feel-ings chance to share my life
JO+SAM
and to find the mean-ing
Pno.
Vc.
Vn.

V.
I know it won't be long 'cause it' ll be today to
I know it won't be long 'cause it' ll be to-day to
Pno.
Vc.
Vn.
day - - - - - to day to
day to day - - - - to
Pno.
Vc.
Vn.

day

# The Girl on T.V.

SARAH

8
V.
- ets      and don't show the class      ets      that  you    can    be  -
Pno.
Vib.

13  ♩=140
V.
tall                                                        when I
Pno.
Vib.

17
3
V.
start-ed at this school I just knew - I just knew that I would fly high well
Pno.
Vib.
20
V.
high-er than the rest so I stu-died the num - bers all the notes and all the books but each
Pno.
Vib.

23
V.
time there's an as - ign - ment it's just one thing in my way of the
Pno.
Vib.
25
V.
hopes and dreams I fight for in class ev - ry sing - le day all the
Pno.
Vib.

27
V.
Pno.
Vib.
hopes that one day I could may-be   stand up tall and   say - - - i'm   that

31
V.
Pno.
Vib.
girl on T. V.   who de - liv - ers the weat - her   I   know you're im-pressed by my coll -

V.
ect-ion of sweat-ers   I   wake up real ear - ly point at   screens and share lists      it is
Pno.
Vib.

Sarah:
We have clear and sunny Skys ahead for Sarah...
V.
me   -   -   -   your met-i-or-tol-o-gist
Pno.
Vib.

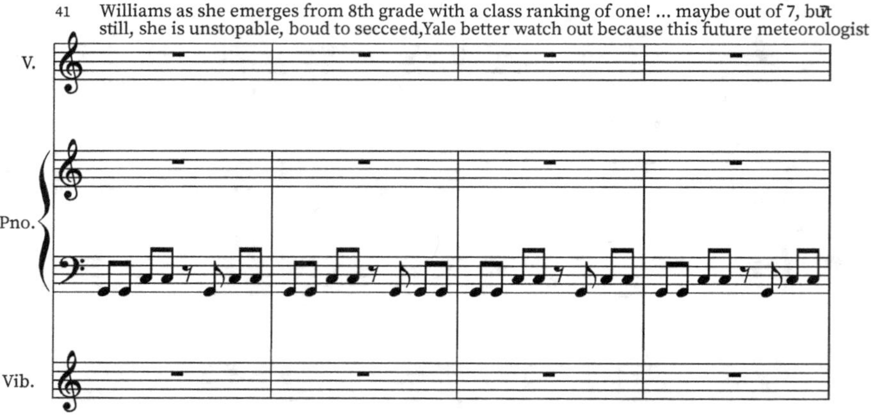

41
Williams as she emerges from 8th grade with a class ranking of one! ... maybe out of 7, but
still, she is unstopable, boud to secceed,Yale better watch out because this future meteorologist
V.
Pno.
Vib.


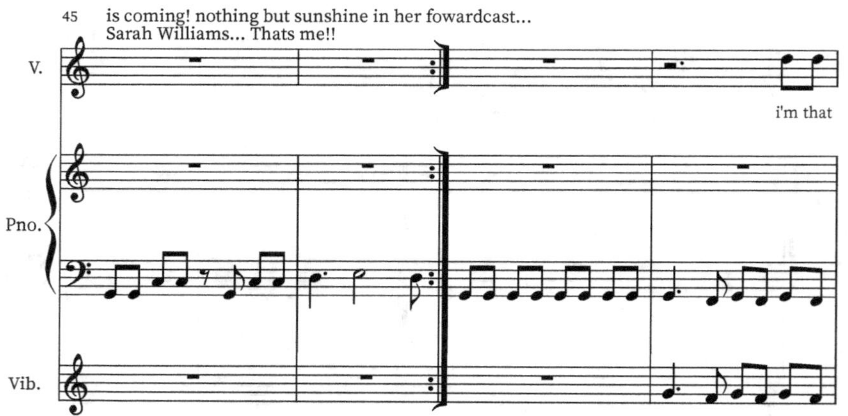

45
is coming! nothing but sunshine in her fowardcast...
Sarah Williams... Thats me!!
V.
i'm that
Pno.
Vib.

49
V.
girl on T.V.   who de - liv - ers the wea - ther   I   know   it feels weird tp know a
Pno.
Vib.
52
6
V.
loc - al ce - leb - ri - ty   but   im here   I can help you through the win - ter sum - er
Pno.
Vib.

56
V.
snow rain and cra-zy weat-her when to wear a coat and when to wear a sweat-er
Pno.
Vib.
59
V.
'cause it will be me when you need a met-i-or-ol-o-gist
Pno.
Vib.

gist - - - - - - gist-

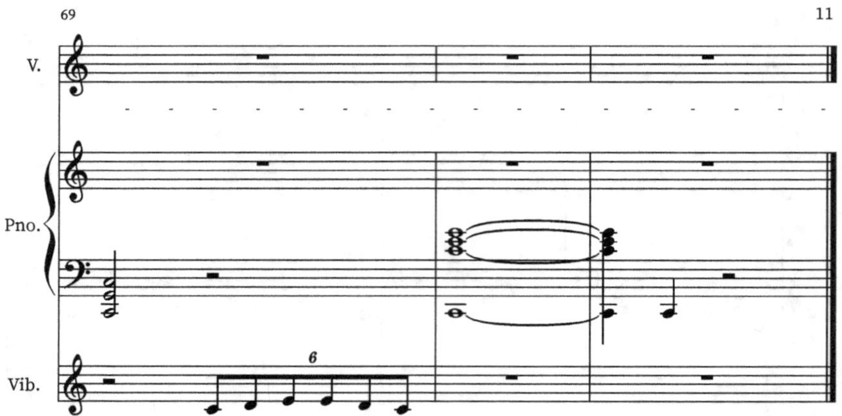
V.
Pno.
Vib.
6

# The Bug Song

Maisie & Sam

V.
V.
Pno.
Pno.
Vc.
I'm
6
6

V.
norm' - ly not the type to just talk a - loud but I think this is a
V.
Pno.
Pno.
Vc.

V.
chance for me to step up and talk ab-out what it is that makes me me operatic
V.
Pno.
Pno.
Vc.
mp

Maisie: Get it, like the note mi (laughs)
like do, re, mi... anyways...
V.
mi
V.
Pno.
Pno.
Vc.

pen pal I think we could be best of friends not like I have man - y

V.
but I think that through all these lett-ers we      can   be,      can   be - e-cause
V.
Pno.
Pno.
Vc.

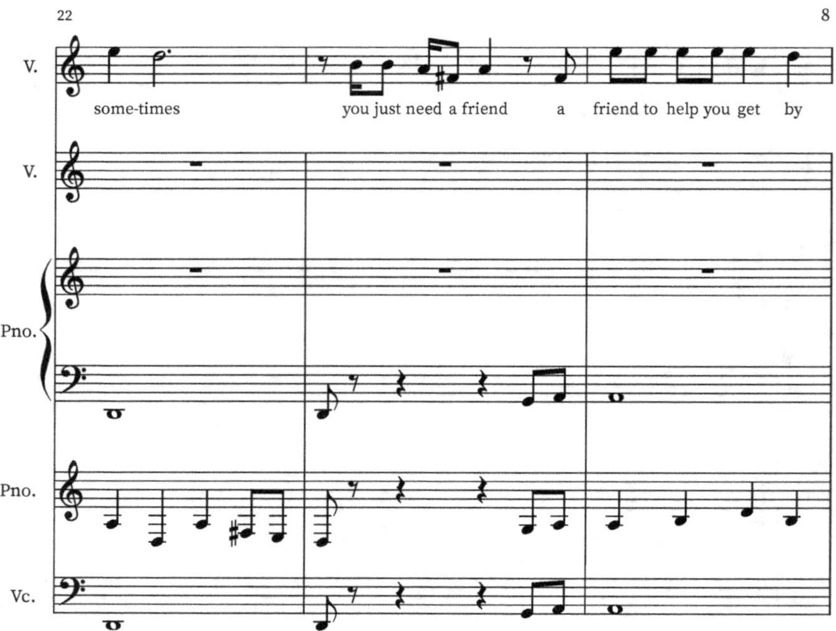
some-times
you just need a friend a friend to help you get by
V.
V.
Pno.
Pno.
Vc.

to the ver - y end     a    spec - ial frien
to  be there for me

what do you think?

V.
V.
Pno.
Pno.
Vc.
I

real - ly like bugs and I like to go for walks I like to sit in the sun

I spend all my days drawing pict-ures of bugs that

(INSERT LONG BUG JOKE)

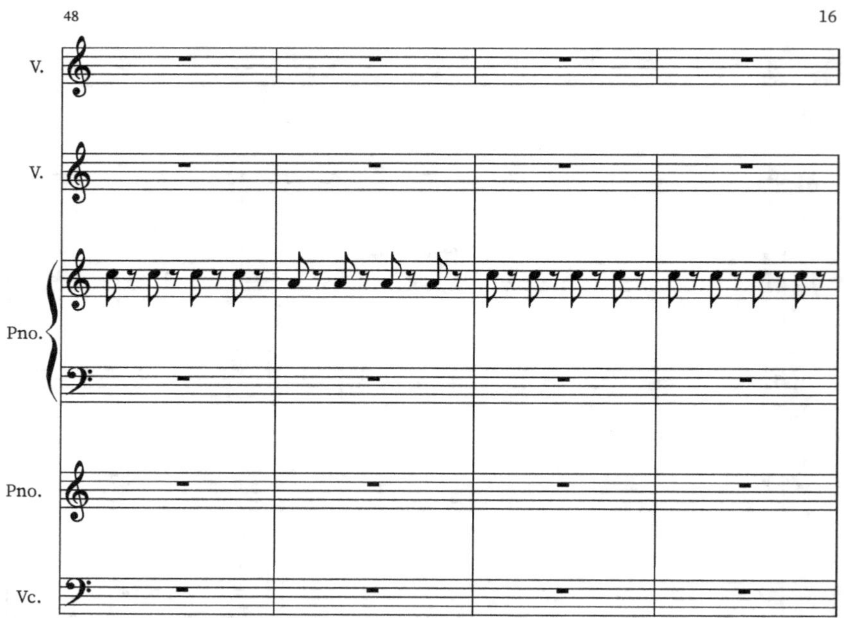

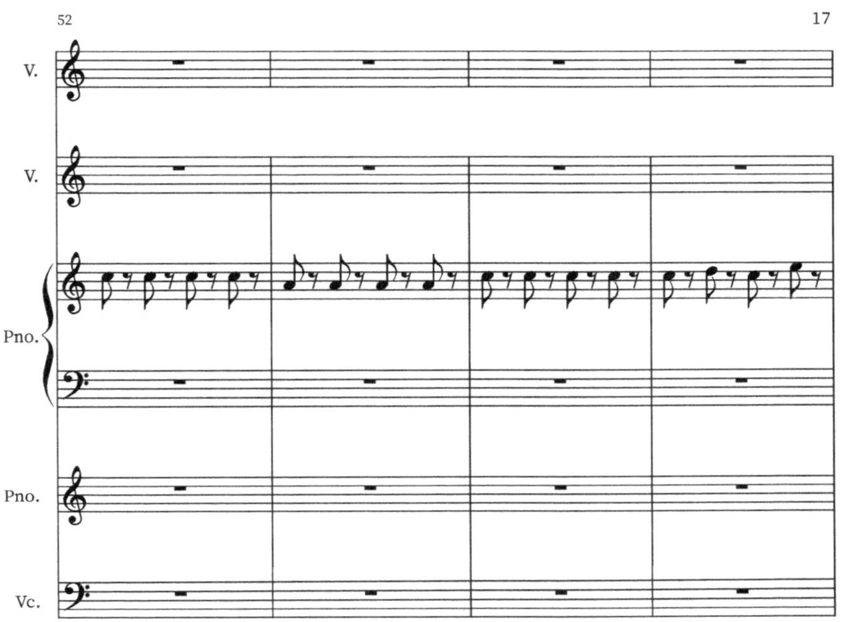

so, you got an - y hobb-ies?
bugs

64   MAISIE        SAM          MAISIE                    20
V.
and  in your free time   I   like bugs   sure - ly theres gott-a be   more  to you
V.
Pno.
Pno.
Vc.

V.
with  pict-ures    of    bugs  -    -
MAISIE
V.
cause
Pno.
Pno.
Vc.

bu - - - ugs
I love
some-times
you just need a friends
a
friend to help you get by

bugs bu - ugs bu - ugs bu -
to the ver - y end a spec - ial friend to be for me e e

- ugs so - me times bu - - -
e e e some-times you kust need a friend a friend to help you get by

V.
gs                    i real-ly like      bu  -    -    -    ugs

V.
to the very    end           a      spec - ial friend        to  be there for you and  to

Pno.

Pno.

Vc.

help you find
more bugs
help you find the mean-ing of life
the mean-ing of

more bugs bu - - - - -
life the mean-ing of life - - - -

V.
ugs
V.
Pno.
Pno.
Vc.
6
6
6
3

# The Girls I Didn't Love.

Liam

V.
park-ing lot
we hit  it off
like two peas in  a  po-
Pno.
Dr.
Vn.

9
V.
Pno.
Dr.
Vn.
- - - - - d      but when she  said good-bye      I
12
said "see you lat-er" to   find out that Kate   was a      pea hat-er so I   head-ed home    and

V.
now I know that she's just one     of the girls     I     thought I  loved but act' ly
Pno.
Dr.
Vn.
20
V.
did'-nt  love yeah she's just one     of the  girls     I     loved
Pno.
Dr.
Vn.

then there was Grace, stu-dent-bod - y pres-i-dent

V.
Pno.
Dr.
Vn.
she had the face    of Mar-i lyn mon-roe - e - - - e    So I

gave her some dia-monds, a
girl' best friend    to    find out that there was a

noth-er ma - n    so I    swing and I miss and I    add  to  the list    of the

44
V.
Pno.
Dr.
Vn.
girl - - s I thought I loved but act'-ly did'-nt love yeah she's just
48
V.
Pno.
Dr.
Vn.
one of the girls I loved but then there's

her the girl who reads my let - ters I
know it's weird but there's a conn - ect - ion here yes she's that

girl - - - - - - - - - I read from write to and
love yeah, she's not one of the girl - s I

65
13
V.
though I loved but act'ly did'-nt love no she's a girl - - - - l I
Pno.
Dr.
Vn.
69
V.
love
Pno.
Dr.
Vn.

V.
Pno.
Dr.
Vn.

# Speechless

Sky

such a hard thing to do
well not for you

I write all these stor - ies I spend all my time I

15
V.
pour out my heart - and soul in ev - ery line but ev - ery time I speak I
Pno.
Vc.

18
V.
feel im not there I talk but it seems you don't
Pno.
Vc.

V.
care - - - - - cause you snick - er and laugh and you call
Pno.
Vc.
22
V.
me a fool you push me a-round and use me as a to - ol I
Pno.
Vc.

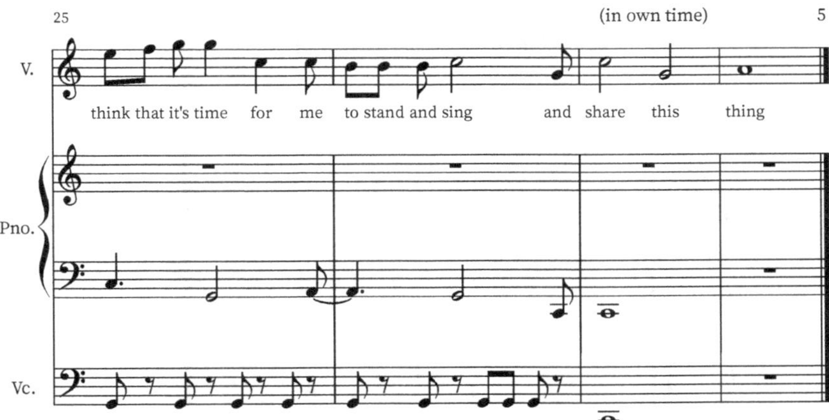
25
(in own time)
V.
Pno.
Vc.
think that it's time for me to stand and sing and share this thing

# The Binder Song.
### Ensemble

SARAH                                    MAISIE

Pno.

Pno.

Vc.

Vn.

wish I was dream-ing or this was some sort of prank but it's there it's right there and
Pno.
Pno.
Vc.
Vn.
Maisie: Hey! let's be smart here, is that really the BEST idea I mean-
now I wan-na
Pno.
Pno.
Vc.
Vn.

look at it! noth-ing is tell-ing us no so

17
Pno.
why don't we just pick it up and give it a go - It's sitt-ing right there and look-ing
Vc.
Vn.
20
LIAM
Pno.
lone-ly and scared and I am sing-le as can be and I am turn-ing the big one-three and this is
Vc.
Vn.
3

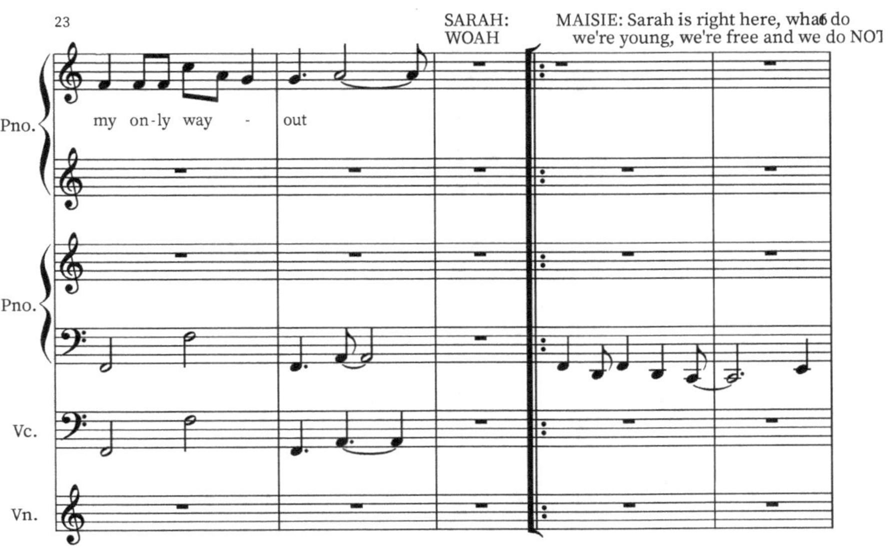
SARAH:
WOAH
MAISIE: Sarah is right here, what do
we're young, we're free and we do NOT
my on-ly way - out
Pno.
Pno.
Vc.
Vn.

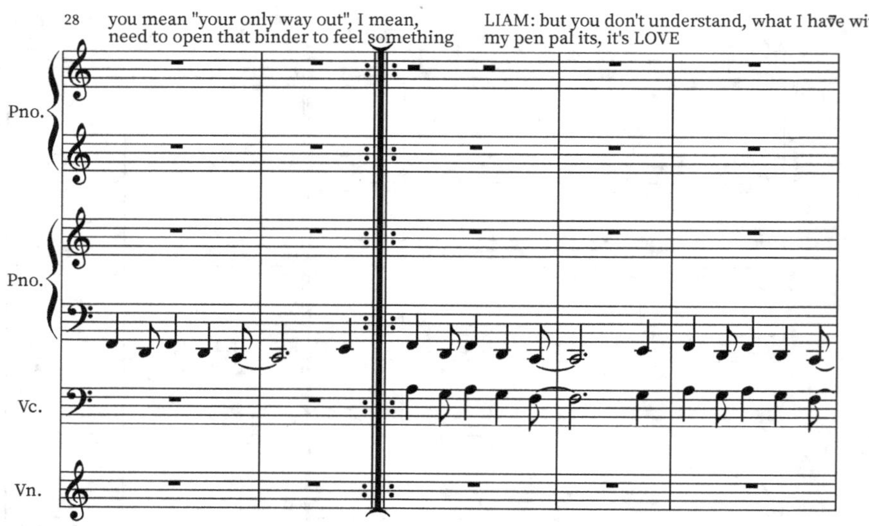

28
you mean "your only way out", I mean,
need to open that binder to feel something
LIAM: but you don't understand, what I have with
my pen pal its, it's LOVE
Pno.
Pno.
Vc.
Vn.

LIAM: I mean, I know it sounds crazy but this is different
than anything I've ever had before, she is different
cause i'm to young for Grace or I am
Pno.
Pno.
Vc.
Vn.
1.
2.

too short for Lizz-ie but my pen pal right here thinks that I am the shizz-y my

Pno.
pe - e - n pal  it's like she  fin-al-ly sees me  my  pe - en  pal
Pno.
Vc.
Vn.

44  SKY:
I mean what's to say your pen pal is a "she"..
LIAM: BLEH
JO: I mean, is there something wrong with that?
Pno.
Pno.
Vc.
Vn.

49
LIAM: no, no, it's not that, it's just, it's just...
I don't know what to think...
Pno.
Pno.
Vc.
Vn.
ser-i-ous-ly    have we

Pno.
tried our  best?    we
run the risk of  su-spen-sion by
just cross-ing this desk    I
Pno.
Vc.
Vn.

Pno.
think it'd be bet - ter if we just sit down but there are sec-rets that are kept that will stay
Pno.
Vc.
Vn.

qui-et if not lept at by this opp - ot-tun - it - y - y - - - so

may-be we don't ms.
rup - us seems bu - sy and you
think that I care? hey list - en

Pno.
up "mis-ter shi-zzy"-we should just stay - calm and for - get this whole thing cause
Pno.
Vc.
Vn.

they can't know

they can't know

I

others

no - vels po - ems

Pno.

Pno.

Vc.

Vn.

wish they could they can't know it'd do me no good but
lies chance to share my feel - ings chance to share my life and to fing the mean-ing

77
I know it wont be long   cause it will be   to-day
to
Pno.
Pno.
Vc.
Vn.
81
day   to - day
to
Pno.
Pno.
Vc.
Vn.

# The Girls I Didn't Love. (Reprise)

Liam

V.
Pno.
Vc.
Dr.
Glock.
see my plan all a - long has fin - 'ly sho - own my sis - ter my sis - ter HA look

V.
Pno.
Vc.
Dr.
Glock.
at that though    cause I knew all  a - long   so  I  said let's  be strong

V.
Pno.
Vc.
Dr.
Glock.
let's be wrong ans trick her   thats what I  did                    yeah your're just

V.
one     of the girls     YOU thought I loved but act'-ly did'nt  love ni you're just
Pno.
Vc.
Dr.
Glock.

one of the girls I thought I loved but act'ly did'-nt love no you're not

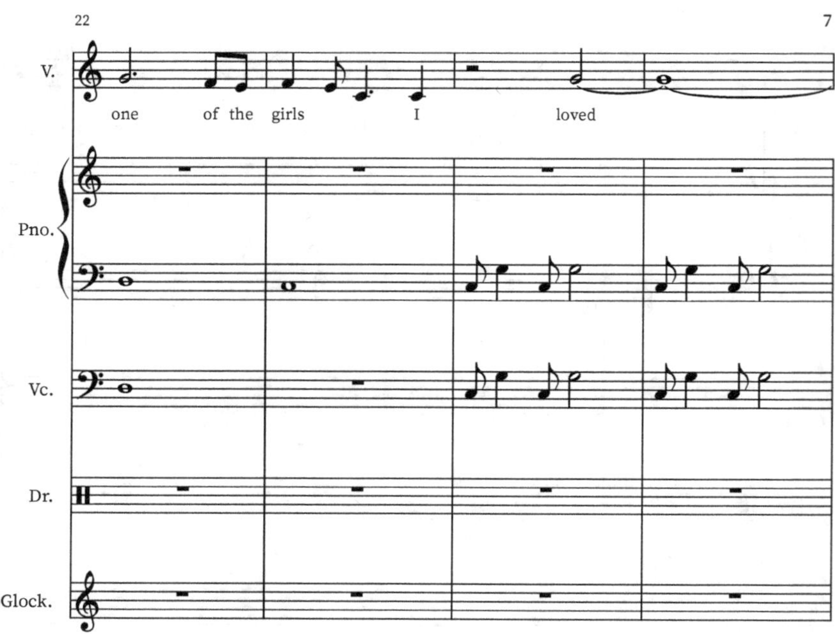
one    of the  girls        I            loved

# Starting Over.
Ensemble

4
1.
Maisie
V.
V.
V.
Pno.
Vc.
I    have an old soul    I    don't talk to stran-gers    I

sit  in  the back      I    learn names and face - s      I     don't talk too lou - d      I

keep to my-self I     I try    so - o hard

V.
V.
V.
Pno.
Vc.
for you to see     I'm     her   -   -   e     I

V.
V.
V.
Pno.
Vc.
try to just be what you nee - d me to be - but now I see thay you don't

care so this is when we all should just start ov - er the

point we should for - get who we we - re      who we are      and who   we're try'ng

to be
just for - get a-bout the things we have sai -

d      for they were  said when we were in      our  he - a - d - s   so  let it just be

Li - am and Sar - ah and Jo Sky Ty Sam and me

39
♩ = 120
Sarah
V.
I
V.
V.
Pno.
Vc.

V.
think Mai-sie's rig - ht   lets give it  a whirl     cause there are things you don't know
V.
V.
Pno.
Vc.

V.
V.
V.
Pno.
Vc.
bout this cool girl      I      like  to chase storm clouds   put   them in  my book       then

when the storms ov - er it just takes a look to know I can be the

great-est met-e-or-ol-o-gist in His tor-r - y  I  can  see - e

V.
V.
V.
Pno.
Vc.
bright ans sunn-y skies for    me  -    -  so    this  is  the time   we should all -

V.
- start ov - er    and   share who we   real - ly  are          share who we      wan -
V.
V.
Pno.
Vc.

V.
V.
V.
Pno.
Vc.
t - ed to be and if we've - got-ten far                    for

V.
get a - bout the things that we said - - for they were said when we were in
V.
V.
Pno.
Vc.

+LIAM    +MAISIE    +JO 21
our  hea - d    so  let  it  just be    Li - am and Mai - sie ans Jo

V.
Sky  Ty  Sam
i'm sec-ret-l - y  lac -
V.
V.
Pno.
(CAST CLAPPING WITH BEAT)
Vc.

tos  in - tol - er - ant    that's why  I  don't like cheese
he    don't    like  cheese

V.
I wan-na move to san fran sis - c - o though I don't like the beach
V.
V.
Pno.
Vc.

V.
I on-ly like bugs cause of my dead mom
V.
no no no beach
V.
Pno.
Vc.

86
26
V.
her fav'-rit bug was a lad - y bug
ALL
I GOT THESE sec - rets that
V.
V.
Pno.
Vc.

i can't hi - de    I    like    to    eat    cheese
LIAM
I    HAD    a    pet frog that    i    acc - a - dent - all - ly
ALL OTHERS
these lett - ers    I    thought    were    pre - et - ty

(JO blurts out his secret).
Character of choice:
Woah me too!
V.
fries
V.
killed
V.
great
(vamping)
Pno.
Vc.
so

this is the time when we all - start ov - er    and share who we have been all  a long

g    share who we    wan - t ed to be who we thin - k that we are -    - e
want - ed    to    be    think    that    we    ar -    e

for - get ab - out the things that we sai - d     for they were
for     get ab - out the things that we said     for they were

104
32
V.
said when we were in our he - ads so let it just be -
V.
said when we were head so let it just be
V.
Pno.
Vc.

li - am and Sar - ah and Jo - Sky ty Sam Mai -

V.
i - sie the sec - rets and thing - we held in cause - we can fin - all ly
V.
V.
Pno.
Vc.

be free and be
you you you you you you you you
V.
V.
V.
Pno.
Vc.

115
rit.
V.
you you you and me!
V.
V.
Pno.
Vc.

# Finale.

Ensemble

V.
ooo - wah we shared the nov - els po - ems lies chance to share my feel-ings
Pno.
Vc.
Vn.
Glock.

chance to  share  my   life  and to find the mean-ing  chance to real-ly share

V.
Pno.
Vc.
Vn.
Glock.
who I want to be - e-cause We know it won't be long be-cause we did today

to day
to -

V.
day
to - day
Pno.
Vc.
Vn.
Glock.

23
V.
Pno.
Vc.
Vn.
Glock.